"WHY WAS I ADOPTED?"

Books in this delightful series...

"WHERE DID I COME FROM?" by Peter Mayle and Arthur Robins.
The facts of life without any nonsense.

"WHAT'S HAPPENING TO ME?" by Peter Mayle and Arthur Robins.
A guide to puberty, from the authors of "WHERE DID I COME FROM?"

"WHY DO I HAVE TO WEAR GLASSES?" by Sandra Lee Stuart and Arthur Robins.

"WHY AM I GOING TO THE HOSPITAL?" by Claire Ciliotta, Carole Livingston, and Dick Wilson. A helpful guide to a new experience.

"WHY DO WE NEED ANOTHER BABY?" by Cynthia MacGregor and David Clark.
Puts to rest fears and quells the anxieties for new-baby-to-be's brothers and sisters.

"WHY WAS I ADOPTED?" by Carole Livingston and Arthur Robins.
The facts of adoption with love and illustrations.

"WHAT AM I DOING IN A STEPFAMILY?" by Claire Berman and Dick Wilson.
How two families can be better than one.

HOW TO BE A PREGNANT FATHER by Peter Mayle and Arthur Robins.
An illustrated survival guide for the father-to-be.

Each book is delightfully written and complete with full-color illustrations!

Ask for these books at your local bookseller. Or order directly from the publisher by calling 1-800-447-BOOK. Also, be sure to ask for our complete catalog of titles: Carol Publishing Group, 120 Enterprise Avenue, Dept. 40400, Secaucus, NJ 07094.

You'll be glad you did!

"WHY WAS I ADOPTED?"

Written by Carole Livingston. Illustrated by Arthur Robins.
Designed by Paul Walter.

For Jennifer.
With special thanks to Claire Berman.

Carol Publishing Group Edition, 1996

A Lyle Stuart Book
Published by Carol Publishing Group
Lyle Stuart is a registered trademark of Carol Communications, Inc.

Editorial, sales and distribution, rights and permissions inquiries
should be addressed to Carol Publishing Group, 120 Enterprise Avenue,
Secaucus, N.J. 07094

In Canada: Canadian Manda Group, One Atlantic Avenue, Suite 105,
Toronto, Ontario M6K 3E7

Carol Publishing Group books may be purchased in bulk at special
discounts for sales promotions, fund-raising, or educational purposes.
Special editions can be created to specifications. For details, contact
Special Sales Department, Carol Publishing Group, 120 Enterprise Avenue,
Secaucus, N.J. 07094

Manufactured in the United States of America
ISBN 0-8184-0400-0

15 14 13 12 11 10 9 8 7 6

Library of Congress Cataloging-in-Publication Data

Livingston, Carole.
Why was I adopted?
SUMMARY: A simple explanation of the facts of adoption.
1. Adoption—Juvenile literature. [1. Adoption]
I. Robins, Arthur. II. Title.
HV875.L53   362.7'34   78-5111

Let's start at the beginning.

<u>What are you?</u>

Well, it's easier to say what you are not. You're not a gorilla. You're not a puppy dog. You're not a mouse. And you're certainly not a rhinoceros.

You're a human being. A person. One of the many people on this earth. There are more than three and one half billion like you – and yet you are different from every one of them.

You're unique because you're you!

Well, we know <u>what</u> you are, but the big question is <u>who</u> you are.

<u>Who are you?</u>

You know your name, don't you? It's different than your best friend's name. But that doesn't make you different from all the other people because <u>some</u> of them may have a name just like yours.

You probably can guess some of the things that are the same about you and all of those other people in the world.

For example, almost everyone has two eyes, two ears, two legs and a mouth.

But there are plenty of ways that you are different too.

Not all of us have the same color eyes or hair or skin. Some of us are tall and some short. Some are chubby and some skinny. Some are as old as 102½ and some are as young as a two minute baby.

Let's talk about that baby for one minute.

You know of course that the baby didn't come out of a chewing gum machine or in a package that the postman delivered. Nor did it grow on a tree or bush.

That's it!

People may be all sizes, shapes, ages and they may be rich or poor or live in cold countries or hot countries but they all have one thing in common.

Every single one of them had a mother and a father!

That mother and father gave you a very special gift. It's so special that no one else can ever give it to you and so special that even they can give it to you only once.

They gave you the gift of life.

By giving you the gift of life, they gave you your birthday. And every year on the same day you can get kisses and hugs from your family and your friends and they can all sing Happy Birthday to you. (And you get a birthday cake and presents too.) Birthdays are lots of fun, aren't they?

Now we come to the serious part.

Serious doesn't mean unhappy. It just means important. Important for you, that is.

The thing is that sometimes something may happen so that the family you began with is not the same as the family you have now.

You said what?

We'll repeat it. Sometimes the family you began with isn't the same as the family you have now.

Hmmmmm…that certainly sounds serious!

There are so many different things that might have happened that we couldn't list them all even in a book ten times this size!

But let's take a few possibilities.

Like: maybe your birthfather and birthmother were still so young themselves (remember you were a baby then) that they could not know how to give you the care and attention you need because they had so much growing up to do themselves.

That's a funny thought! (Who'd want to be brought up by a couple of other children?)

Or, your birthmother or your birthfather – or maybe even both of them – may have died. That's very sad, isn't it?

And these are only two of the many reasons why the parents who gave you your birthday are different from the parents you have now.

What all of this means is that if you are an adopted child, you became part of your family in a different way than by just being born into it.

You were wanted by somebody very, very much.

They wanted you!

(Not a bad choice! They must be pretty smart!)

Now, remember all those differences we talked about earlier, like different hair color, eye color, and so on? Well, if you're adopted, you have something else that not every kid has. You have birthparents (the ones who gave you your birthday) and you have adoptive parents (the ones who love you now and wanted you very, very much.)

In some ways you're pretty lucky.

An "adoptive parent" is a special kind of person. Not just any grown-up can be one.

The most important thing about them is that an adoptive parent really loves children and wants a child very much.

That's how your parents came your way. They wanted to care for you and love you and help you grow up.

Pretty nice of them isn't it?

Pretty lucky for you too, isn't it?

Come to think of it, pretty lucky for them that they got you!

But don't start getting stuck up!

Stuck up children sometimes have their noses so high in the air they don't see the floor and trip over a French poodle or slip on a banana peel!

Also, a lot of people, including other children don't like stuck-ups!

So let's face it. Being adopted is lucky and happy but it doesn't mean you're better than anybody. It doesn't make you smarter or cuter or bigger.

You still have to go to bed when you're told and brush your teeth and eat your spinach and carrots.

Being adopted doesn't mean you don't have to do your homework either.

Being adopted _is_ a special difference. We'll admit that. But being able to stand on your head is pretty special too, isn't it?

You're not the only child who has ever been adopted. Millions of people were adopted. You may even have friends who were adopted.

Or maybe your sister or brother was too.

There are lots of famous people who were adopted too.

Two of our former presidents were adopted: Herbert Hoover and Gerald Ford.

But most of the people who are adopted aren't famous.

So, in some ways, being adopted is like belonging to a gigantic club. Even though the reasons for adopting each child may be different, there's one thing that's the same. This is so important we're going to say it all alone on a separate page.

Adoptive parents adopt children because they want them very, very much.

Your parents wanted <u>you</u> very, very much.

Then why does Daddy yell sometimes when you don't eat your vegetables? Or Mommy become angry if you sit too long in front of the TV?

Being adopted doesn't mean never getting yelled at. Of course not.

And why do you slam your door sometimes when you're angry at them?

Being adopted doesn't mean never being angry with your family. And it doesn't mean being perfect, you know. (What a perfectly ridiculous idea <u>that</u> is!)

What it means is that when all the feelings are put aside, your Mom and Dad wanted you and needed you and love you.

And let's let them in on the secret: you want them and need them and love them too. It's a pretty good arrangement, isn't it?

You bet it is!

Do you wonder where people go to adopt children?

Well, they don't go to the zoo. They don't go to a super-market either. Did you ever see a sign in a store window that said "Kids for Sale!"?

Not very likely!

You don't find children in Crackerjack boxes either! Actually, every adoption is different and each child is adopted in a different way.

Some people go to agencies that know where there are children who need families.

The people who work in these agencies try very hard to find out if people who ask to be parents really understand about the hard parts as well as the fun.

Sometimes, if your birthparents died or were unable to care for you, you might have been adopted by your Aunt and Uncle or your Grandparents. Or maybe an older sister or brother.

Or, sometimes doctors or lawyers know people who want to adopt a child and they help get them together with a child who needs a home.

Some parents already have children who are born to them but they may have decided they wanted more children and they knew about kids who needed parents. So they adopted one. Or two. Or three. Or four!

Often a woman and a man are unable to have children (it happens many times) and they want a child so much they aren't really happy until they have one.

Some kids live in other countries where there may have been lots of bad problems.

Maybe a famine – not enough food to feed everyone. Or a war with lots of horror – certainly no place for children. (Or grown-ups either!)

In cases like these, children are sometimes put into an airplane and flown to their new parents.

They may not even speak the same language – unless they are babies. (And we all know that babies can only say "goo goo" and gurgle – no matter <u>where</u> they are born. Babies can sound very much alike in every language.)

Sometimes people end up with kids who look a lot like themselves. But sometimes they don't.

There are so many ways of adopting children, it can be very confusing.

People who adopt children don't mind it if life gets a little mixed up.

Sometimes just one person adopts a child. Then that one person has to do the job of both mother and father. And that makes a family too.

It's all pretty complicated, isn't it? But pretty interesting too.

Your parents can tell you exactly how and why they wanted a child and happened to adopt <u>you</u>.

Okay, do you still have some questions?

No surprise! We thought this might happen and so we talked to lots of other children who were adopted.

They had questions, too. We thought you'd want to know some of the things they asked us.

Take a deep breath...Here goes!

<u>I was so little when I was adopted that I can't remember my birthparents. Is that okay?</u>

Sure. Most children don't recall things that happened when they were very little, so how could you be expected to remember your birthparents? You probably can't remember what you ate for lunch last Wednesday...

If you were bigger when you were adopted you may know more about your birthparents. That's okay too. You may even want to keep a special family scrapbook starting with what you remember as long ago as possible.

Can people really pick out the child they want?

Well, not usually. Sometimes they know the child they are going to adopt, but most of the time they have to be just as surprised as any other parents who have a new child.

Does it cost a lot of money to adopt a child?

It may cost a lot – or nothing at all. Sometimes just being there when somebody wants a child is all it takes.

What if my parents don't like me? Can they send me back and maybe get a new kid?

No way! Adoption is forever. Laws are very strict about that. And don't forget – your parents adopted you because they wanted you.

Supposing I get angry and change my mind?

Sorry. You've got to stick with it.

Do my parents love me more or less than my brother or sister who isn't adopted?

Being adopted doesn't make any difference in the way people love. They love you all very much.

What about my birthparents? If they're still alive and know where I am, can they just come along one day and take me back?

No. Laws are very strict about this too. You belong to your adoptive parents now and they belong to you.

Do I have sisters and brothers from my birthparents that I don't know about? Or maybe aunts and uncles?

It's possible. Sometimes your parents don't even know this. But if you do, you'll have an even larger family than most kids!

What if I want to know more about my birthparents?

Your curiosity is natural. Talk about it with your Mom and Dad.

Sometime in your daydreams you may imagine that your birthmother was a famous ballet dancer and your birthfather was a famous medical doctor. More likely they were very much just like your folks now.

When I grow up will I have adopted children?

When you grow up you can decide.

Why did my parents tell me I was adopted?

They want to be open and honest with you. Just as they expect you to be honest with them.

There's one thing that should be said that isn't a question or an answer. One of the most important things to happen to your parents (the ones you have now) was adopting you. It was one of the most exciting and happy events in their lives.

<u>Now that I know all this, what does it all mean?</u>

As we said earlier, you're not prettier, or smarter or bigger or smaller. What it means is that your parents wanted a child very, very much and that child is you and you're all pretty lucky!

Your parents are now your real Mom and Dad because they're the Mom and Dad who take care of you and love you.

In other words, being adopted means being a member of a family... <u>your</u> family.

From time to time you may have other questions. You may wonder about other things. Don't be shy. Ask! Sometimes your folks won't know the answers themselves (parents aren't perfect, though they're <u>almost</u> perfect!) but if they do, they'll tell you.

And they may have a few questions to ask you too!